Gambling and Gaming Addictions in Adolescence

by
Mark Griffiths

Series Editor
Martin Herbert

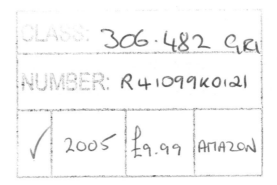

BPS Blackwell

© Mark Griffiths 2002
A BPS Blackwell book

THE BRITISH PSYCHOLOGICAL SOCIETY
St Andrews House, 48 Princess Road East, Leicester LE1 7DR

BLACKWELL PUBLISHING
350 Main Street, Malden, MA 02148-5020, USA
9600 Garsington Road, Oxford OX4 2DQ, UK
550 Swanston Street, Carlton, Victoria 3053, Australia

First published 2002 by The British Psychological Society and Blackwell Publishing Ltd

2   2005

Library of Congress Cataloging-in-Publication Data

Griffiths, Mark, 1966–
    Gambling and gaming addictions in adolescence / by Mark Griffiths.
        p. cm. —(Parent, adolescent, and child training skills 2 ; 13)
    Includes bibliographical references and index.
    ISBN 1-85433-348-8 (pbk. : alk. paper) — ISBN 1-85433-359-3 (set : alk. paper)
    1. Teenage gamblers. 2. Compulsive gambling. 3. Video games and teenagers.
4. Compulsive behaviour in adolescence. I. Title. II. PACTS series—Parent, adolescent, and child training skills 2 ; 13.

HV6710 .G75 2002
363.4′2′0835—dc21

                                                                    2002066736

ISBN-13: 978-1-85433-348-3 (pbk. : alk. paper)

A catalogue record for this title is available from the British Library.

Set in Lapidary
by Ralph J. Footring, Derby
Printed and bound in the United Kingdom
by TJ International, Padstow, Cornwall

The publisher's policy is to use permanent paper from mills that operate a sustainable forestry policy, and which has been manufactured from pulp processed using acid-free and elementary chlorine-free practices. Furthermore, the publisher ensures that the text paper and cover board used have met acceptable environmental accreditation standards.

For further information on
Blackwell Publishing, visit our website:
www.blackwellpublishing.com

Gambling and Gaming Addictions in Adolescence

Books are to be returned on or before
the last date below.

- - APR 2009

LIBREX —

Parent, Adolescent and Child Training Skills 2
Series Editor: Martin Herbert

Contents

Gambling and gaming addictions in adolescence

Introduction

Aims

The aims of this guide are to provide the practitioner with:

- an understanding of why children and adolescents may come to play fruit machines and videogames to excess;
- knowledge about the risk factors for this;
- some practical and common-sense interventions that may be beneficial for such children and adolescents;
- some practical advice to give to their parents.

Objectives

To fulfil these aims, the guide will help a practitioner:

- to explore the literature on the excessive playing of fruit machines and videogames by children and adolescents;
- to assess the impact of such behaviour;
- to think through with parents matters arising from it;
- to plan interventions.

Part I: Behavioural addictions

For many people, the concept of addiction centres on drugs. However, there is now a growing movement (e.g. Orford, 1985) which views many behaviours as potentially addictive, including gambling, overeating, sex, exercise and playing computer games, and this has led to new, all-encompassing definitions of what constitutes addictive behaviour. One such definition is that of Marlatt *et al.* (1988, p. 224), who define addictive behaviour as:

> a repetitive habit pattern that increases the risk of disease and/or associated personal and social problems. Addictive behaviours are often experienced subjectively as 'loss of control' – the behaviour contrives to occur despite volitional attempts to abstain or moderate use. These habit patterns are typically characterized by immediate gratification (short term reward), often coupled with delayed deleterious effects (long term costs). Attempts to change an addictive behaviour (via treatment or self initiation) are typically marked with high relapse rates.

While, most people have their own idea of what constitutes 'addiction', actually trying to define it can be difficult. It is rather like defining 'mountain' or 'tree' – there is no single set of criteria that can ever be necessary or sufficient to define all instances. When it comes to addiction, the whole is easier to recognize than the parts.

Part II: Technological addictions

Technological addictions are a subset of behavioural addictions which involve excessive human–machine interaction (Griffiths, 1995a). They can be either passive (e.g. television) or active (e.g. computer games) and usually contain inducing and reinforcing features which may contribute to the promotion of addictive tendencies. The category of technological addictions contains addictive activities that could be located under other kinds of addiction. For instance, addiction to playing fruit machines is also quite clearly a type of gambling addiction.

There is little in the way of an established academic literature on technological addictions but activities that could be included under this category are addictions to:

➤ television;
➤ computers (e.g. hacking, programming);
➤ the Internet (e.g. chat rooms, fantasy role playing, surfing);
➤ video and computer games;
➤ fruit machines;
➤ pinball;
➤ trivia quiz machines;
➤ mobile phones;
➤ telephone sex.

To determine whether technological addictions are genuinely addictive, they should compared against the clinical criteria for established addictions. This method of making behavioural excesses more clinically identifiable has been proposed for two potential technological addictions – 'television addiction' (McIlwraith *et al.*, 1991) and 'amusement machine addiction' (Griffiths, 1991a, 1992). Griffiths (1996a, 1996b) has postulated that addictions consist of a number of common components. These components are outlined below.

Salience. This is when the particular activity becomes the most important activity in someone's life and dominates that person's thinking (preoccupations and cognitive distortions), feelings (cravings) and behaviour (deterioration of socialized behaviour). For instance, even if not actually engaged in the behaviour the person will be thinking about the next time he or she will be.

Mood modification. This refers to the subjective experiences that people consistently and reliably report as a consequence of engaging in the particular activity and can be seen as a coping strategy (i.e. they may experience an arousing 'buzz' or a 'high' or paradoxically tranquillizing feel of 'escape' or 'numbing'). Interestingly, people can use the same activity or substance to achieve different effects at different times. For instance, alcohol (a depressant) and nicotine (a stimulant) can both be used for either their arousing or tranquillizing effects by users.

Tolerance. This is the process whereby increasing amounts of the particular activity are required to achieve the former effects. For instance, a gambler may gradually have to increase the size of the bet to experience the euphoric effect that was initially obtained with a much smaller bet.

Withdrawal symptoms. These are the unpleasant feelings and physical effects which occur when the particular activity is discontinued or suddenly reduced (e.g.'the shakes', moodiness, irritability, sweating hands, feelings of nausea, stomach cramps).

Conflict. This refers to the conflicts between addicts and those around them, conflict between the addiction and other activities, such as job or schoolwork (inter-activity conflict) or from within the individual themselves (intrapsychic conflict), when they may experience a subjective loss of control.

Relapse. This is the tendency for repeated reversions to earlier patterns of the particular activity to recur. Even the most extreme patterns typical at the height of the addiction can be quickly restored after many years of abstinence or control.

It can therefore be argued that if any behaviour (e.g. playing fruit machines or videogames) fulfils these criteria then that behaviour should be defined as an addiction.

Part III: Adolescent gambling

Adolescent gambling is a growing problem. It appears to be related to high levels of problem gambling generally and other delinquent activities such as illicit drug taking and alcohol abuse (Griffiths and Sutherland, 1998). It has been noted that adolescents may be more susceptible to pathological gambling than adults. For instance, in the UK, Fisher (1992) found that among adolescent fruit machine gamblers, 6% did so to a pathological degree. Further studies in the UK have revealed a general pathological gambling rate of 5–6% among youngsters under 18 years of age. This figure is two to three times higher than that identified in the adult population (Fisher, 1992; Griffiths 1995b). On this evidence, young people are clearly more vulnerable to the negative consequences of gambling than adults.

Pathological gambling appears to be a primarily male phenomenon (Griffiths, 1991a, 1991b). It also appears that adults may to some extent be fostering adolescent gambling. For example, a strong correlation has been found between adolescent gambling and parental gambling (Griffiths, 1995b; Wood and Griffiths, 1998). This is particularly worrying because a number of studies have shown that when people gamble as adolescents, they are then more likely to become problem gamblers as adults (Fisher 1992; Griffiths, 1995b).

Other factors that have been linked with adolescent problem gambling include working-class youth culture, delinquency, alcohol and substance abuse, poor school performance, theft and truancy (Fisher, 1992; Griffiths 1994a, 1995b; Yeoman and Griffiths, 1996; Griffiths and Sutherland, 1998). However, many of the research findings have not differentiated between different types of gambling. There appear to be three main forms of adolescent gambling that have been widely researched (particularly in the UK) – gambling on lotteries, gambling on scratchcards and on fruit machines. However, the most problematic appears to be gambling on fruit machines and this is the type of gambling that is concentrated on here.

Part IV: Gambling on fruit machines

If I wasn't actually gambling I was spending the rest of my time working out clever little schemes to obtain money to feed my habit. These two activities literally took up all my time. ('Joe')

Gamble, gamble, gamble your life away … you might as well have put it down the drain. You've got to face the truth that you're having a love affair, and it's with a machine whose lights flash, takes your money and kills your soul. ('Gary')

During four or five years of compulsive gambling I think I missed about six or seven days of playing fruit machines – keeping in mind that about four or five of those days were Christmas days where it was impossible to gain access to a gambling machine.… As you have probably gathered, I ate, slept and breathed gambling machines.… I couldn't even find time to spend with the people I loved.… The machines were more important than anything or anyone else. ('David')

There is no doubt that, for some children and adolescents, fruit machines are the most important thing in their lives, as the quotes above demonstrate. A few individuals will play on a fruit machine at least once a day, and even when they are not actually playing them they are thinking about the next time they do. As players become addicts, they become socially withdrawn and start to lose their friends – even the closest ones. Eventually the fruit machine becomes the addict's *best friend*. To reiterate one of the quotes above – 'You're having a love affair, and it's with a machine'. An addict can talk to the machine, shout at it, laugh at it – and it *never* answers back. The machine can make addicts forget their problems, it can arouse them and occasionally even pays them money for being there. In essence, the hard-core player 'worships' the fruit machine.

There is little doubt that fruit machines are potentially addictive – a large body of research worldwide supports this. In the past 10 years, fruit machines have been the predominant form of gambling by pathological gamblers treated in self-help groups and professional treatment centres across Europe (see Griffiths and Wood, 1999, for a comprehensive review of the European literature). There are many reasons why this is the case. Slot machines have high event frequencies (i.e. they are fast action games), aurally and visually stimulating and rewarding, require a low initial stake, provide frequent wins, require little knowledge to play them and may be played alone.

Clearly, decisions to play fruit machines and to continue playing them to excess are contingent upon the player's biological and psychological constitution and situational variables. However, fruit machines are designed to induce the player to play and to continue playing. It has further been argued (Griffiths, 1993a) that a combination of their technological aspects (event frequency, the near miss, light and sound effects, etc.) may contribute towards habitual and repetitive play in some individuals.

Most research on fruit machine gambling in youth has been undertaken in the UK, where they are legally available to children of any age. Fisher and Balding (1998) found that fruit machines were the most popular form of adolescent gambling: among their sample of nearly 10,000 adolescent, 75% had tried in it. A more thorough examination of the literature (Fisher, 1992; Fisher and Balding, 1998; Griffiths, 1995b) indicates that:

➤ at least two-thirds of adolescents play fruit machines at some point in their adolescent lives;
➤ one-third of adolescents will have played fruit machines in the last month;
➤ 10–20% of adolescents play at least once a week;
➤ up to 6% of adolescents are probable pathological gamblers or have severe gambling-related difficulties.

All studies have reported that boys play on fruit machines more than girls and that as playing becomes more regular it is more likely to be a predominantly male activity. Research has also indicated that very few female adolescents have gambling problems on fruit machines.

Reasons for the addiction

But why do adolescents play fruit machines? This is not easy to answer, as there is a host of possible reasons. However, research does suggest that irregular ('social') gamblers play for different reasons than the excessive ('pathological') gamblers.

Social gamblers usually play for the following reasons:

➤ for fun and entertainment (as a form of play);
➤ because their friends or parents do (as a social activity);
➤ for the possibility of winning money;
➤ because it provides a challenge;
➤ because of ease of availability and there is little else to do;
➤ for excitement (the 'buzz').

Pathological gamblers appear to play for other reasons, such as:

➤ mood modification;
➤ a means of escape.

Appendix 1 gives a diagnostic checklist to identify problem gambling in children and adolescents. Not everyone who plays fruit machines will become addicted (in the same way that not everyone who drinks alcohol will become an alcoholic), but, given a cluster of factors (genetic or biological predisposition, social upbringing, psychological constitution, situational and structural characteristics), a small proportion of people will, unfortunately, experience severe problems.

Negative consequences

Like other potentially addictive behaviours, an addiction to playing fruit machines causes the individual to engage in negative behaviours such as truanting in order to play the machines, stealing to fund the habit, getting into trouble with teachers and parents over their machine playing, borrowing or using school dinner money to play the machines, poor schoolwork and in some cases aggressive behaviour (Fisher and Balding, 1998; Griffiths, 1995b). These behaviours are not much different from those experienced as a consequence of other types of adolescent problem gambling. Furthermore, fruit machine addicts also display bona fide signs of addiction, including withdrawal effects, tolerance, salience, mood modification, conflict and relapse.

External factors in adolescent gambling

Griffiths (1999) has noted that there is no precise frequency level of a gambling habit at which people become addicted, since addiction will be the result of a variety of factors, of which frequency is just one. The other factors external to the gamblers themselves which influence the acquisition, development and maintenance of gambling behaviour include:

➤ stake size (is the activity affordable and is it perceived as value for money?);
➤ event frequency (time gap between each gamble);
➤ amount of money lost in a given time period (which is important in 'chasing' – see below);
➤ prize structures (the number and value of prizes);
➤ probability of winning (e.g. 1 in 14 million on the National Lottery);

> size of jackpot (e.g. over £1 million on the National Lottery);
> skill and pseudo-skill elements (whether actual or perceived);
> 'near misses' (the number of near winning situations);
> light and colour effects (e.g. the flashing lights on fruit machines);
> sound effects (e.g. use of buzzers or musical tunes to indicate winning);
> social or asocial nature of the game (individual or group activity);
> accessibility to the venue (e.g. opening times, membership rules);
> geographical accessibility (e.g. number of outlets);
> location of gambling establishment (e.g. out of town, next to workplace);
> type of gambling establishment (e.g. betting shop, amusement arcade);
> advertising (e.g. the amount of promotion through television commercials);
> the rules of the game (easy or hard to understand?).

Each of these factors may have implications for the gambler's motivations and, as a consequence, the social impact of gambling. The ability of any of these factors to induce gambling will depend on an individual's own psychological factors (e.g. reinforcement), and do not influence gambling behaviour independently.

The types of adolescents who play fruit machines to excess

In the UK, there have to date been only two longitudinal observational studies of adolescents who gamble on fruit machines (Fisher, 1993; Griffiths, 1991b). Both studies highlighted the different kinds of player, though they were carried out independently of each other and had somewhat different aims. A closer examination of the two studies reveals a number of striking similarities in addition to a few subtle differences. Griffiths' study examined, from a psychological perspective, both participation and non-participation in 33 UK arcades over 28 months. The basic aim was to gain an insight into the adolescent subculture of amusement arcades. Fisher's study involved, from a sociological perspective, non-participant observation supplemented with formal interviews of arcade clientele, carried out over 14 months while she worked as a part-time cashier in a seaside amusement arcade. Fisher's basic aim was to present a sociological account of arcade fruit machine playing among adolescents. Her analysis was presented in the form of a typology outlining five different types of players:

> arcade kings;
> machine beaters;
> rent-a-spacers;

➢ action seekers;
➢ escape artists.

These were differentiated by their primary orientation towards the fruit machine itself. To compare the findings of the two studies, Fisher's player types are outlined and contrasted with the findings of Griffiths.

Arcade kings

Fisher reported that arcade kings were males in their late teens or early twenties, had some skill in playing fruit machines, played in groups with younger boys (9–10-year-olds) (called 'apprentices') and were unlikely to have problems with their playing (i.e. to become 'addicted'). Their primary motivation for gambling on fruit machines was for a positive gain in reputation. She reported that the groups were coherent and self-supporting with a shared sense of quasi-professional status, and the shared losses and winnings, thus demonstrating group commitment and trust. Additionally the arcade kings shared their 'skills' with the apprentices, who in return performed menial tasks for the kings (e.g. getting money from the change counter).

Griffiths (1991b) also described 'experienced/skilful players' (i.e. the arcade kings) and 'subordinates' (i.e. the apprentices). Griffiths reported that many of the groups (usually three to six members) in amusement arcades had a hierarchy. The belief of high skill in playing fruit machines produced 'skilful' players, who were given a high status by the other members of the group. Sometimes the high-status individuals were just the older members of the group, who, like the 'skilful' players, could interrupt the playing of subordinate group members to give 'advice' (which often meant actually playing for them).

Characteristics of the arcade kings
(Fisher and Bellringer, 1997)

Arcade kings typically:

➢ are male;
➢ are in their late teens or early twenties;
➢ play individually but part of a coherent self-supporting group;
➢ have a motivation for status based on high expenditure, high skill and being 'cool';
➢ are not likely to chase losses;
➢ gamble relatively large amounts;
➢ are likely to pool winnings and knowledge with other 'kings';

➢ memorize the reels;
➢ spend time in 'training sessions';
➢ are undemonstrative in play;
➢ maintain discipline and self-control in play;
➢ will leave a machine unlikely to pay out;
➢ portray emotional stability.

Machine beaters

Fisher reported that machine beaters were males who played alone (because they did not like being watched). Their primary motivation was asocial and was simply to beat the machine. Additionally, it was reported that machine beaters had a propensity to experience 'addictive' problems with their playing. Their determination to beat the machine at any cost required enormous resources of time and money and could lead to unsocial or illegal behaviours.

Similarly, Griffiths (1991b) reported that the motivation for a small minority of players was either to 'beat the machine' or 'beat the system'; this could be achieved in any way possible, including cheating. However, Griffiths believed these players to be a subset of the 'experienced' players (i.e. arcade kings), but this time those who played alone rather than in groups; the machines give these players a sense of mastery, control, competence and achievement.

Characteristics of machine beaters (Fisher and Bellringer, 1997)

Machine beaters typically:

➢ may be 'skilled' and 'know the reels';
➢ play alone;
➢ are fascinated by the workings of the machine;
➢ are motivated by interaction with the machine;
➢ are preoccupied with game techniques;
➢ will play until money runs out;
➢ resent presence of other players;
➢ cannot sustain self-discipline;
➢ chase losses;
➢ lack patience;
➢ cannot control emotions;
➢ manage money poorly;
➢ are determined to beat the machine;
➢ will miss work/college/school to continue playing

> deprive themselves of other needs to keep money for the machine;
> are often remorseful and self-deprecating;
> are likely to become obsessed;
> are problem gamblers or at high risk of becoming one.

Rent-a-spacers

Fisher reported that rent-a-spacers were teenage females with no playing skills and little interest in acquiring them, and who gambled on fruit machines primarily to gain access to the arcade venue, where they could socialize with their friends. Their preferred role was one of 'spectator'.

A similar picture was reported by Griffiths: up to half of all those in the arcade in the evening were 14–18-year-old teenagers of either sex who tended to use the arcade as a meeting place for their social group; playing was predominantly male-oriented with girl(friend)s looking on in 'cheerleader' roles.

Characteristics of rent-a-spacers (Fisher and Bellringer, 1997)

Rent-a-spacers typically:

> are predominantly teenage females;
> have no machine-playing skills;
> have little motivation to acquire machine-playing skills;
> play to gain access to the arcade;
> go to the arcade to socialise with friends;
> have a motivation to meet friends and explore gender role;
> think of the venue as a meeting place;
> play machines to avoid being asked to leave.

Action seekers

Fisher reported that the primary orientation of action seekers was the thrill and excitement of playing. She made no reference to the typical age and sex of this type of player or to whether they usually played alone or in groups.

As with the machine beaters, Griffiths believed action seekers to be a subset of 'experienced' male players in their teens or early twenties (i.e. arcade kings) and described a particular type of regular player whose primary motivating reasons for playing were for excitement, to show off his skill to his friends and to show control.

Characteristics of action seekers (Fisher and Bellringer, 1997)

Action seekers typically:

➤ are motivated by excitement, thrill and tension;
➤ get a 'buzz' from the flow of adrenalin;
➤ are attracted to the rapid cycle of wagering, anticipation and release;
➤ have their excitement of gambling enhanced by feeling like an adult when gambling;
➤ enjoy arcades that allow freedom from parental surveillance;
➤ are also attracted by the deviant activities in some arcades;
➤ are attracted to the dangerous atmosphere of the 'forbidden';
➤ may be a problem gambler or at risk of becoming one.

Escape artists

Fisher reported that escape artists can be either male or female; they were depressed and socially isolated, gambled primarily as a means of escape from overwhelming problems. She also reported that the attraction of fruit machines for escape artists was found in both the game and the venue. The machine was found to be both totally absorbing, so that problems were temporarily forgotten, and provided a source of non-human interaction.

Both Fisher and Griffiths described the machine as an 'electronic friend'. The venue fostered the escape from reality by providing a surreal environment and an opportunity to be among people without the need for intimate social interaction. Griffiths reported that, for some players, the machines could be used as an escape to 'take your mind off things', to 'forget about home' and to relieve depression.

Selnow (1984) reported similarly that addicts used videogames as 'electronic friends'. This assertion had been tested experimentally by Scheibe and Erwin (1979), who studied the conversations of people playing videogames. Out of 40 subjects, spontaneous verbalizations were frequent and recorded in 39 cases, averaging one comment every 40 seconds. They reported widespread use of pronouns for the machine, such as 'it hates me', 'he's trying to get me' or 'you dumb machine', but interestingly no use of the pronoun 'she'. The remarks themselves fell into two categories – direct comments to the machine and simple exclamations or expletives. Scheibe and Erwin concluded that players were reacting to videogames as if they were people. This has also been found in experimental studies of people playing fruit machines (Griffiths, 1994b).

Characteristics of escape artists (Fisher and Bellringer, 1997)

Escape artists typically:

➢ are motivated by a need to escape from overwhelming problems;
➢ are usually depressed and may be socially isolated;
➢ feel powerless and lack control;
➢ get a feeling of power by playing machines;
➢ are attracted to both playing machines and the venue;
➢ find the arcade atmosphere aids the escape from reality;
➢ find the arcade provides an opportunity for non-intimate social contact;
➢ are attracted to machines as a source of non-human interaction;
➢ find the machine provides an 'electronic friend';
➢ forget their problems as the machine interaction is totally absorbing;
➢ get a temporary feeling of control by playing on machines;
➢ are problem gamblers or are at a high risk of becoming one;
➢ have gambling almost certainly as a secondary problem;
➢ will cease gambling after resolution of the primary problem.

Conclusion

Despite being from different theoretical perspectives, with differing method-ologies and differing aims and objectives, the two independent studies are conceptually very similar. The biggest difference in the typologies outlined is that Griffiths believes machine beaters and action seekers to be hierarchical subgroups of arcade kings, although Fisher does admit that her categoriz-ations may not be mutually exclusive. The 'experienced' type of player that Griffiths described subsumes the aforementioned three types without trying to distinguish between each, as the motivations of action seeking, trying to beat the machine and the gaining of social rewards appear to be highly interlinked. Since both authors independently identified what appear to be two distinct types (i.e. escape artists and rent-a-spacers), it may be that these particular types are mutually exclusive. The implications of this typology for intervention and treatment are discussed in a later section.

Risk factors for adolescent gambling on fruit machines

One consequence of the recent upsurge in research into adolescent gambling is that we can now start to put together a 'risk factor model' to describe those individuals who might be at the most risk of developing pathological gambling tendencies. Based on the preceding overview and previous summaries of the empirical research literature by Griffiths (1995b), a number of clear risk factors in the development of problem adolescent gambling emerge. Adolescent problem gamblers are more likely:

➢ to be male;
➢ to have begun gambling at an early age (as young as eight years);
➢ to have had a big win earlier in their gambling careers;
➢ to chase losses;
➢ to gamble on their own;
➢ to have parents who gamble;
➢ to be depressed before a gambling session;
➢ to have low self-esteem;
➢ to use gambling to cultivate status among peers;
➢ to be excited and aroused during gambling;
➢ to be irrational (i.e. have erroneous perceptions) during gambling;
➢ to use gambling as a means of escape;
➢ to have bad grades at school;
➢ to engage in other addictive behaviours (smoking, drinking alcohol, illegal drug use);
➢ to come from the lower social classes;
➢ to have parents who have a gambling (or other addiction) problem;
➢ to have a history of delinquency;
➢ to steal money to fund their gambling;
➢ to truant from school to go gambling.

There are also some general background factors that might increase the risk of an adolescent becoming a problem gambler (Bellringer, 1999). Common factors include:

➢ a broken, disruptive or very poor family;
➢ difficult and stressful situations within the home;
➢ a heavy emphasis on money within the family;
➢ the death of a parent or parental figure in childhood;
➢ serious injury or illness in the family or him/herself;
➢ infidelity by parents;
➢ high incidence of abuse (verbal, physical or sexual);
➢ feeling of rejection as a child;
➢ feelings of belittlement and disempowerment.

This list is probably not exhaustive but incorporates what is known empirically and anecdotally about adolescent problem gambling. As research into the area grows, new items will be added to the list while factors, signs and symptoms already on these lists will be adapted and modified.

How to identify when gambling has become a problem

Gambling has often been termed 'the hidden addiction' (Bellringer, 1999; Griffiths, 1995b), because:

➤ There are no observable signs or symptoms, unlike in other addictions (e.g. alcoholism, heroin addiction);
➤ Money shortages and debts can be explained away with ease in a materialistic society.
➤ Adolescent gamblers do not believe they have a problem or wish to hide the fact.
➤ Adolescent gamblers generally become very adept at lying.
➤ Adolescent gambling may be only one of several excessive behaviours.

Although there have been some reports of a personality change in young gamblers (e.g. Griffiths, 1989), many parents may attribute the change to adolescence itself (evasive behaviour and mood swings, for example, are commonly associated with adolescence). It is quite often the case that many parents do not even realize they have a problem until their son or daughter is in trouble with the police.

Griffiths (1995b) reported that there are warning signs to look for although, individually, many of these signs could be put down to adolescence. However, if several of them apply to a child or adolescent they could suggest that there is a gambling problem. The signs include:

➤ no interest in school, highlighted by a sudden drop in the standard of schoolwork;
➤ unexplained free time such as going out each evening and being evasive about where they have been;
➤ coming home later than expected from school each day and not being able to account for it
➤ a marked change in overall behaviour (that perhaps only a parent would notice, such as becoming sullen, irritable, restless, moody, touchy, bad-tempered or constantly on the defensive);
➤ constant shortage of money;
➤ constant borrowing of money;
➤ money missing from home (e.g. from mother's purse or father's wallet);
➤ selling personal possessions and not being able to account for the money;

> criminal activity (e.g. shoplifting in order to sell things to get money for gambling);
> coming home hungry each afternoon after school (because dinner money has been spent on gambling);
> loss of interest in activities they used to enjoy;
> lack of concentration;
> a 'couldn't care less' attitude;
> lack of friends or falling out with friends;
> not taking care of their appearance or personal hygiene;
> constantly telling lies (particularly over money).

However, many of these 'warning signs' are not necessarily unique to gambling addictions and can also be indicative of other addictions (e.g. alcohol and other drugs).

Confirming that gambling is indeed the problem may prove equally as difficult as spotting the problem in the first place. Directly asking adolescents if they have a problem is likely to lead to an outright denial. Talking with them about their use of leisure time, money and spending preferences, and their view about gambling in general, is likely to be more effective. Appendices 2 and 3 list the early warning signs of a possible gambling problem and some definite signs, while Appendix 4 gives a thumbnail profile of a problem gambler.

Opportunities for change

There are some specific 'trigger' situations and circumstances in which a gambling problem can first come to light. Bellringer (1999) highlights an array of situations that provide an opportunity to help gamblers focus on a need to change. These are:

> *Acceptance by gamblers that control has been lost* – this is the step before they ask for help.
> *Asking for help* – having realized for themselves that gambling has taken control over their life, they may reach out to those closest to them.
> *Observation of too much time spent in a gambling environment* – such observations by friends or family may provoke discussion as to how this is affecting the life of a gambler.
> *Getting into financial trouble and accumulating debts* – this might be a crisis point at which problem gambling raises its head for the first time.
> *Uncovered lies* – these may lead to admissions of gambling problems.
> *Dwindling social circles and the loss of close relationships* – these may again lead to problem gambling being discovered by family or friends.

> *Discovered crime* – this is usually a real crisis point when the family may discover the truth for the first time.
> *Homelessness* – being thrown out of the family home may be the trigger for problem gamblers to be honest for the first time about the mess they are in.

What can parents do?

Discovering that you are the parent of an adolescent problem gambler can be highly stressful – particularly as it is often a problem that parents feel they have to face on their own. Before getting involved with their children, parents have to understand the problem as well as the *process* of problem gambling. By the time a young gambler acknowledges there is a problem, the family may have already gone through a lot of emotional turmoil, including feelings of anger, sadness, puzzlement and guilt. Parents should try to get in touch with a helping agency as soon as possible (helpful addresses are given in Appendix 5). The Hints for Parents section on p. 54 gives a list of points for parents either during or as a follow-up to their initial contact with a helping agency (Bellringer and Farman, 1997).

Practical interventions for adolescents addicted to playing fruit machines

Psychologists have used many different types of treatment for people with a gambling problem. These include various forms of psychotherapy, behavioural therapy, cognitive-behavioural therapy, as well as various forms of counselling and self-help therapies. These will not be discussed here, as the focus will be on practical interventions.

For adults, one of the first ports of call is often the local Gamblers Anonymous (GA) group (see Appendix 5 for an address). A question that is often asked is whether GA can help young gamblers. The honest answer is that it can do so only sometimes. There are many reports in the literature about how hard it is for children and adolescents to attend such meetings. There are obviously distinct advantages and disadvantages. The factors which may facilitate attendance at GA include:

> the young gambler's desperation and fear about the gambling situation;
> legal pressure;
> parental pressure;
> a parent attending GA with the youngster;
> seeing GA as a way out of financial crisis;
> realizing that others recognize the problem;

> the friendly atmosphere;
> the opportunity to learn about the destructive results of compulsive gambling.

There are, however, many reasons why adolescents may not like attending GA meetings. These include:

> forced attendance;
> lack of transport;
> the fact that meetings may clash with social life;
> the generation gap between members;
> different important life factors;
> a fear of the unknown;
> the lack of relevant literature to their age group;
> not being able to relate to the emphasis on self-help;
> the meetings being perceived as authoritarian;
> being in a minority (i.e. they may be the only young person there at the meeting).

It appears that intervention and treatment for adolescents need to be more practical and pragmatic. As we saw earlier, there appear to be different types of fruit machine player, with differing characteristics. Therefore, there may be slightly different interventions based on their primary motivation for gambling. This knowledge can also be used for diagnosing or addressing the primary problem(s) that lie behind their gambling. While each player type describes the dominating motivation to play, they are not necessarily mutually exclusive. The machine beaters, escape artists and action seekers appear to be the most likely to develop gambling problems. However, the boundary line between them and the social gambler are fluid. Caution must be exercised before reaching conclusions about particular types of player, as it is quite possible that individuals shift between player types and that predominant characteristics can change quickly.

There has been little in the way of treatment approaches specifically geared towards adolescents. However, there is one programme that has been designed in the UK to help specifically in the treatment of adolescent gamblers. This is a non-theoretical approach called 'Ten Key Aspects' and outlined by Bellringer (1993). The 10 aspects come under two categories (*Preparation* and *Action*) and are described below in more detail. A brief summary for practitioners is also given in Appendix 6.

Preparation

1. Understanding the issues
2. Structure change

Action

3. Assessing the problem
4. Providing counselling
5. Developing trust
6. Building self-esteem
7. Providing support
8. Managing finances
9. Developing interests
10. Measuring progress

(1) *Understanding the issues* involves practitioners asking themselves questions to get an idea of the adolescent gambler's situational context. How does gambling become a problem for some people? How can the danger signs be spotted? Who else could help this particular gambler's rehabilitation? Some questions may have no direct answers but by asking the question, practitioners can at least get insight into some of the issues involved.

(2) *Structure change* involves the setting up of a plan by the practitioner and adolescent gambler, with realistic goals and measurable objectives. The exact mechanism for a structure for change is negotiated between the practitioner and the adolescent gambler but essentially involves three stages:

➤   *diagnosis* – initial assessment of the problem, identifying objectives and ensuring that they are attainable and measurable;
➤   *design* – considering options available to meet objectives, discussing costs and benefits of options;
➤   *action* – agreeing how objectives will be achieved, deciding on the strategy to be employed, carrying through the plan.

(3) *Assessing the problem* is self-explanatory and involves a more in-depth assessment of the adolescent's gambling problem. The practitioner at this stage needs to assess:

➤   whether the client's gambling really is a problem;
➤   who the gambling affects;
➤   how the gambler and significant others view the problem;
➤   the extent to which the gambler is motivated to stop;
➤   the underlying motives for their gambling;
➤   whether the problem gambling is primary or secondary.

Assessing whether the gambling problem is primary or secondary is quite important as this may save a lot of time in the therapeutic process. For instance, the two case studies reported below (from Griffiths, 1991c) highlight the theme of secondary addiction as an 'escape' from a distressing environment to one of 'control' in another (the amusement arcade) in fruit machine addicts. These cases highlight that the excessive fruit machine gambling was a secondary problem caused by the underlying main problem of feeling out of control in the family environment. By addressing the primary problem (i.e. the family environment), the secondary symptoms (i.e. the excessive fruit machine playing) disappeared.

> A 12-year-old boy lived with his divorced mother, an 18-year-old sister and a 17-year-old sister (both of whom had a different father from the boy). The household was thus feminine, with make-up, dresses and other female items scattered about the place, and the mother and the sisters all entertained different male friends fairly regularly. In this environment the boy felt completely alien and sought solace in an environment in which he thought he could cope (the arcade) and have power (over a fruit machine). The mother was advised to let the boy live with his father, which she did, and the gambling problem stopped.

> A 17-year-old boy lived with his father and stepmother. Their family home was very plush and expensive and the family was very materialistic. Inside the home he was afraid to walk on the carpet (the pile was so deep), afraid to put a cup on the table (it was so highly polished), and so on. The boy felt completely alien to this sort of environment. Again, it was an environment in which he had no control; therefore, he sought out an environment to which he thought he could escape (the arcade) and have power over something (the fruit machine). He was advised to leave home. Although he still visited his family after moving out, his gambling stopped.

(4) *Providing counselling* has the object of empowering adolescent gamblers to effect change for themselves. Important considerations at this stage are agreeing the boundaries (i.e. staying within the boundaries of the agreed contract), creating the right atmosphere (i.e. counselling to be provided in a comfortable environment free of interruptions) and appropriate involvement (i.e. involving the family and other helping agencies where appropriate).

(5) *Developing trust* is a particularly important element of the programme and involves discussing the issue of trust and confidentiality with the adolescent gambler, helping the gambler to trust others and to be open and honest, empowering the gambler to change, avoiding hidden agendas or secret collusion with other people in the gambler's life and providing consistent support to the gambler.

(6) *Building self-esteem* helps to restore confidence. The adolescent gambler's self-esteem will almost certainly be low; therefore, the practitioner must understand the gambling problem from the gambler's perspective and formulate short-, medium- and long-term goals. Where possible the practitioner must attempt to turn negatives into positives and chart the adolescent gambler's progress, thus facilitating a sense of achievement. Criticism should be kept to a minimum and each session should always end on a positive note.

(7) *Providing support* should involve a support agency, the practitioner's agency, other agencies and the adolescent gambler's family, friends and significant others. The family should be brought in to help at the earliest appropriate moment and should, where possible, take an active role in providing additional support to the adolescent gambler. Support is particularly needed after relapses and after the main contact with the gambler has been terminated.

(8) *Managing finances* (i.e. debt counselling) involves a thorough assessment of the adolescent gambler's financial situation and its object is to reduce the stress and despair of money problems. Such actions as talking to creditors, cutting up credit cards and drawing up budget plans are all useful. Getting another family member to take control of the adolescent gambler's expenditure may also be considered as a short-term option but the long-term aim is gradually to give back financial responsibility to the gambler.

(9) *Developing interests* has the objective of replacing the destructive habit with a range of activities that are rewarding in themselves. By finding out what the adolescent gambler likes about gambling, the practitioner may be able to suggest alternatives which give the same kinds of physiological or psychological rewards. This is not as easy as it sounds but should be pursued. Some help may be required in the development of social and life skills.

(10) *Measuring progress* is needed to provide effective feedback to the adolescent gambler. The use of graphs, checklists and diaries may be useful. Self-assessment and measuring success in the gambler's terms as well as the practitioner's may also be useful. The involvement of family and friends where appropriate should be encouraged. Objectives and goals should be revised and reset at regular intervals.

The *Ten Key Aspects* can be used in conjunction with other therapies and could be viewed as either a supplement to other treatment techniques or a process of therapy in itself. Although this programme has yet to be evaluated, many of the aspects outlined are common-sense actions, although formalizing them in a stage-wise fashion may lead to a more coherent approach to the problem.

Relapse prevention

If gamblers have successfully broken a dependency on gambling, it is important that they put in place measures that will help them to prevent gambling relapses. Useful strategies include the following:

➤ they should place a limit on future gambling, or avoid gambling altogether;

➤ they should internalize learning and avoid reverting to ingrained reactions to difficult or stressful situations;

➤ they should watch for situations and circumstances that trigger the urge to gamble and be ready to face them;

➤ they should nurture self-esteem (i.e. work at feeling good about themselves);

➤ they should develop a range of interests that, preferably, meet similar needs to those that were previously being met by gambling;

➤ they should spend time and energy working at building good human relationships;

➤ they should reassess the significance of money and endeavour to reduce its importance in their lives;

➤ they should continue to explore, on occasion, reasons why gambling became so significant in their lives.

Other more general steps that gamblers should be encouraged to do include:

➤ be honest with themselves and others;
➤ deal with all outstanding debts;
➤ accept responsibility for their gambling;
➤ abstain from gambling while trying to break the dependency;
➤ talk about how gambling makes them feel;
➤ take one day at a time;
➤ keep a record of 'gambling-free' days;
➤ be positive and not give up after a 'slip' or a 'lapse';
➤ reward themselves after a gambling-free period;
➤ develop alternative interests.

A self-help guide for young gamblers is given in Appendix 7.

'Good gambling'

Parents and practitioners should also be aware that problems are likely to be avoided when the young gambler keeps in control of the situation and ensures that any gambling remains a social activity. Appendix 8 is a brief guide, based on Bellringer (1999), aimed particularly at young gamblers but is applicable to everyone.

Conclusions

The general public still know little about addiction to the playing of fruit machines. It is possibly true to say that most people consider fruit machines to be a harmless amusement from which people occasionally receive a financial reward. Nevertheless, to a small minority, fruit machines are as problematical, as destructive and as addictive as psychoactive drugs. Although knowledge of adolescent gambling is growing, it is still highly inadequate. The preceding overview has demonstrated that fruit machine addiction is a bona fide addiction which fulfils all the core components of addiction.

Since sociological factors appear to be critical in the acquisition of this addiction, prevention needs to be aimed at the social and situational antecedents. There are a number of levels at which this can be approached (e.g. societal, school, family, individual), some of which may be more practical than others. Since pathological gamblers start playing fruit machines at a significantly earlier age than non-pathological gamblers, an obvious step would be for the UK government to legislate against young people playing fruit machines. A 'blanket ban' on using such machines would thus prevent acquisition until at least late adolescence. Another approach might be to raise awareness of the dangers of fruit machine gambling not only among children and adolescents but also among those who have an influence over them (e.g. parents, guardians, teachers). Although this is unlikely to prevent fruit machine gambling in all young people, it might reduce the total number of adolescents who start to gamble on fruit machines and the amount of time an adolescent spends playing them.

Since many adolescents play fruit machines because of a lack of age-appropriate facilities, it would seem practical to set up youth clubs that, like the arcades, are perceived to be minimally supervised and allow adolescents to be autonomous. The fact that some players are socially rewarded for playing fruit machines cannot be altered directly, but more adaptive personal and social skills can be taught as responses to stress: for example, relaxation, assertion and social skills training. As gambling may be modelled by both parents and peers, the family's role in maintaining gambling behaviour should be addressed in therapy, and any prevention plan should aim to increase the gambler's contact with non-gambling peers.

The studies suggested that players pathologically addicted to fruit machines are not a homogeneous group – there appear to be at least two subtypes of addict. This would have major treatment implications. It has been speculated that one type of gambler appears to be addicted to the fruit machine itself and plays to test their skill, to gain social rewards and most of all for excitement. This is termed a 'primary addiction'. The second type of pathological gambler appears to play fruit machines as a form of escapism, where the machine is possibly an 'electronic friend'. These players are usually depressed, socially isolated and are those who fit the stereotypical 'lone addict' media image. This is termed a 'secondary addiction', in that the player uses fruit machines as an escape from a primary problem (e.g. a broken home or relationship break-up). Such a distinction has obvious clinical usefulness (as suggested by the case examples above).

Finally, before going on to examine videogames, a short section follows which explores the many similarities between fruit machines and video-games.

Part V: Videogames and fruit machines — commonalities

Although there are different licensing laws for different types of gaming machine in the UK, both videogame machines and fruit machines tend to be located in amusement arcades and other single-site premises (e.g. public houses, cafes, fish and chip shops, cinemas, etc.). However, videogames can also be played on a hand-held console, on a home television console and on a personal computer (including over the Internet).

Both videogame machines and fruit machines may be considered under the generic label of 'amusement machines' (Griffiths, 1991a) (see Appendix 9 for the differences between types of gaming machine in the UK). The main difference between videogame machines and fruit machines are that videogames are played to accumulate as many points as possible whereas fruit machines are played (i.e. gambled upon) to accumulate money. Griffiths (1991a) has suggested that playing a videogame could be considered as a non-financial form of gambling. Both types of machine (if arcade-based) require insertion of a coin to play, although the playing time on a fruit machine is usually much less than on an arcade videogame machine. This is because on videogames the outcome is almost solely due to skill, whereas on fruit machines the outcome is more likely to be a product of chance. However, the general playing philosophy of the players of both is *to stay on the machine for as long as possible using the least amount of money* (Griffiths, 1990). Griffiths has argued that many fruit machine players *play with money rather than for it* and that winning money is a means to an end (i.e. to stay on the machine as long as possible).

Besides the generic labelling, their geographical juxtaposition and the philosophy for playing, it could also be argued that on both a psychological and a behavioural level, fruit machine gambling and videogame playing share many similarities (e.g. similar demographic profiles such as age and gender breakdown, similar reinforcement schedules, similar potential for 'near miss' opportunities, similar structural characteristics involving the use of light and sound effects, similarities in skill perception, similarities in the effects of excessive play). The most probable reason the two forms have rarely been seen as conceptually similar is because playing videogames does not involve the winning of money (or something of financial value) and therefore cannot be classed as a form of gambling. However, the next generation of fruit machines are starting to use videogame graphics and technology. While many of these relate to traditional gambling games (e.g. roulette, poker, blackjack) there are plans to developing video gambling games in which people would win money based on their game scores. This gives an idea of the direction in which fruit machines and videogames are heading.

A growing number of researchers suggest that arcade videogames share some common ground with fruit machines, including the potential for dependency. As Fisher and Griffiths (1995) point out, arcade videogames and fruit machines share some important structural characteristics:

➤ the requirement of response to stimuli which are predictable and governed by the software loop;
➤ the requirement of total concentration and hand–eye coordination;
➤ a rapid span of play, negotiable to some extent by the skill of the player (more marked in videogames);
➤ the provision of aural and visual rewards for a winning move (e.g. flashing lights, electronic jingles);
➤ the provision of an incremental reward for a winning move (points or cash) which reinforce 'correct' behaviour;
➤ digitally displayed scores of 'correct behaviour' (in the form of points or cash accumulated);
➤ the opportunity for peer group attention and approval through competition.

As with excessive playing of fruit machines, the excessive playing of videogames partly comes about by the partial reinforcement effect (PRE) (Wanner, 1982). This is a critical psychological ingredient of videogame addiction, whereby the reinforcement is intermittent (i.e. people keep responding in the absence of reinforcement hoping that another reward is just around the corner). Knowledge about the PRE gives the videogame designer an edge in designing appealing games. The magnitude of reinforcement is also important. Large rewards lead to fast responding and greater resistance to extinction – in short, to more 'addiction'. Instant reinforcement is also satisfying.

Part VI: Adolescent videogame playing

Videogames rely on multiple reinforcements (this is the 'kitchen sink' approach to their design) in that different features might reward different types of people. Success on videogames comes from a variety of sources and the reinforcement can be intrinsic (e.g. improving the highest score, beating a friend's high score, getting a name in the 'hall of fame', mastering the machine) or extrinsic (e.g. peer admiration). Malone (1981) has also reported that enjoyment of videogames is positively correlated to:

➢ the presence of goals;
➢ the availability of automatic computer scores;
➢ the presence of audio effects;
➢ the random aspect of the games;
➢ the degree to which rapid reaction times enhance game scores.

Since their introduction in the early 1970s, videogames have become big business. Until very recently, most research on the effects of videogames centred upon the alleged negative consequences (e.g. videogame addiction, increased aggressiveness after playing videogames) – at least in the popular press. In the following sections there is an examination some of the health consequences (both positive and negative) of playing videogames, based on empirical evidence. Compared with the literature on the playing of fruit machines, there is far less available and there is almost nothing on intervention and treatment. As a consequence, the following sections concentrate on what is known.

Videogames are clearly an endemic part of adolescence and on the surface there are many positive reasons why they are played by so many. Most surveys in the UK have shown that a vast majority of adolescents play videogames and that between a quarter and a third play every single day (Griffiths and Hunt, 1995, 1998). Males play videogames significantly more regularly than females. There appear to be three reasons why this may be the case.

1. *The content of the games.* On the whole, videogame software is designed *by* males *for* males. Although some manufacturers have introduced software she-versions of popular male-dominated games (e.g. *Ms. Pac-man*) these have generally been unsuccessful. Even new games with strong female characters like Lara Croft have tended to alienate more females than they have attracted.

2. *Socialization factors.* Another explanation for the gender difference may be socialization. Women have not been encouraged to express aggression in public and are unlikely to feel comfortable with games of combat or war. Research indicates that males prefer to play games for competition and mastery, whereas females prefer more whimsical, less aggressive and less demanding games.

3. *Innate gender differences.* A third factor is that males on average perform better in visual and spatial skills – particularly depth perception and image solving. These skills are essential in good game playing since good hand–eye coordination is needed in addition to the quick judgements of spatial relationships (Keisler *et al.*, 1983). Keisler *et al.* noted that since boys would tend to score higher than girls due to the differences in visual and spatial skills, the girls' average lower scores could be considered a discouraging factor in their reluctance to continue playing videogames.

So what are the attractions of playing videogames? First, those who have a television console can play it in their own home and those who have a handheld console can play it just about anywhere. Furthermore, they do not have to pay for repeated plays like they would at an amusement arcade. Videogames also have the capacity to 'stretch time' and players can play again and again with no predetermined stopping point. The playing of videogames is one of the few activities that children and adolescents can have control over in their lives and, when parents are computer illiterate, it is one world that their parents cannot enter! It is not hard to see why videogames are so popular. Furthermore, it has been argued that videogames improve hand–eye coordination, raise self-esteem and provide a sense of mastery and achievement. Before looking at the possible downside of videogame playing, it is worth pointing out that videogames can indeed be used in positive ways.

The benefits of videogames

Many people seem surprised that videogames have been used innovatively in a wide variety of therapeutic and medical contexts. For instance, 'videogame therapy' has been used successfully as:

➤ a training and rehabilitation aid to cognitive and perceptual/motor disorders such as stroke;
➤ part of cognitive rehabilitation programmes for people with attentional difficulties;
➤ an intervention to promote and increase arm reach in persons with traumatic brain injury;

➤ a form of physiotherapy for arm injuries;
➤ a form of occupational therapy to increase hand strength;
➤ part of a rehabilitation programme to improve sustained attention in patients with craniocerebral trauma;
➤ a technique to train the movements of those with Erb's palsy;
➤ a technique for respiratory muscle training for young patients with muscular dystrophy.

The use of videogames in all these differing contexts capitalizes on the person's motivation to succeed, and has advantages over traditional therapeutic methods which rely on passive, repetitive movements and sometimes painful limb manipulation.

Videogames have also been used in a number of studies as 'distracter tasks'. For instance, one study reported the case of using a handheld videogame (Nintendo GameBoy) to stop an eight-year old boy picking at his face. The child had neurodermatitis and scarring due to continual picking at his upper lip. Previous treatments (e.g. behaviour modification) had failed so a handheld videogame was used to keep the boy's hands occupied. After two weeks with the videogame the affected area had healed.

Specially designed videogames have also been used to increase educational awareness of health-related issues, particularly among children and adolescents.

Therapists working with children have long used games in therapy sessions with their young patients. Play has been a feature in therapy since the work of Anna Freud and Melanie Klein, and has been used to promote fantasy expression and the ventilation of feeling. The recent technological explosion has brought a proliferation of new games which some therapists claim to be an excellent ice-breaker and rapport-builder with children in therapy and behaviour management. Research in the mid-1980s had already suggested that videogames may actually facilitate cooperative behaviour and reinforcement in more educational settings.

Gardner (1991) claimed that the use of videogames in his psychotherapy sessions provided common ground between himself and his client and provided excellent behavioural observation opportunities. According to Gardner, such observations allowed him to observe:

➤ the child's repertoire of problem-solving strategies;
➤ the child's ability to perceive and recall subtle cues as well as foresee consequences of behaviour and act on past consequences;
➤ hand–eye coordination;
➤ the release of aggression and control;
➤ the possession of appropriate methods of dealing with the joys of victory and frustrations of defeat in a more sports-oriented arena;

> the satisfaction of cognitive activity in the involvement of the recall of bits of basic information;

> the enjoyment of mutually coordinating one's activities with another in the spirit of cooperation.

Gardner went on to describe four particular case studies where videogames were used to support psychotherapy and added that although other techniques were used as an adjunct in therapy (e.g. story telling and drawing), it was the videogames that were the most useful factors in the improvement during therapy. It is Gardner's contention that one's clinical techniques tend to change as a function of the trends of the times, though one's goals remain the same. Slower-paced and more traditional activities like those outlined above may lengthen the time it takes to form a therapeutic relationship as the child may perceive the therapist not to be 'cool' or 'with it'.

Videogames: medical and physical effects of excessive play

Having briefly outlined some of the positive benefits of playing videogames, it is worth mentioning that there has been an increasing amount of research on the more negative consequences of videogame play. The risk of epileptic seizures while playing videogames in photosensitive individuals with epilepsy is well established. Graf *et al.* (1994) report that seizures are most likely to occur during rapid scene changes, and with high-intensity repetitive and flickering patterns. However, for many individuals, seizures during play will represent a chance occurrence without a causal link. Abstinence from playing will usually stop the seizures although in extreme cases where this does not occur, medication with anticonvulsants may be used. Further to this, Millett *et al.* (1997) reported that epileptics considerably overestimate the risks of photosensitive epilepsy for themselves. The authors argue that accurate information should be given to every individual with epilepsy regarding their personal susceptibility to photo-induced seizures, so that those who are not at increased risk may participate in relevant activities without undue concern.

There has been a whole host of case studies in the medical literature reporting some of the other adverse effects of playing videogames. These have included auditory hallucinations, enuresis, encopresis, wrist pain, neck pain, elbow pain, tenosynovitis – also called 'Nintendinitis'! – and peripheral neuropathy. Admittedly, some of these adverse effects are quite rare and 'treatment' simply involved not playing the games in question. In fact, in the cases involving enuresis and encopresis, the children were so engaged in the games that they did not want to go to the toilet. In these particular cases they were simply taught how to use the game's 'pause' button!

There has also been some speculation that excessive play may have a negative effect on both heart rate and blood pressure. One study (Gwinup *et al.*, 1983) suggested that some individuals with cardiovascular disease could experience adverse effects. More recent research has highlighted both gender and ethnic differences in cardiovascular activity during game play (Murphy *et al.*, 1995). Although some authors (e.g. Segal and Dietz, 1991) have suggested that game playing may lead to increased energy expenditure when compared with activities such as watching television, the energy increase identified is not sufficient to improve cardio-respiratory fitness.

More recently, Hatch *et al.* (1998) reported a study on 640 patients with leukaemia (with 640 matched controls) and reported that the risk of acute lymphoblastic leukaemia was increased with children's use of both arcade videogame machines and home videogame consoles. However, the patterns of risk for duration of use (in years) and frequency of use were inconsistent for most appliances used by children. This is clearly an area where more research is needed.

Childhood obesity has also been linked with the playing of videogames. For instance, Shimai *et al.* (1993) found that obesity was correlated with long periods of videogame playing in Japanese children. This finding has also been found in young French children (Deheger *et al.*, 1997). In the UK, Johnson and Hackett (1997) reported that there was an inverse relationship between physical activity and playing videogames in schoolgirls.

The main health consequences of excessive videogame playing may be summarized as follows:

➢ auditory hallucinations;
➢ enuresis;
➢ encopresis;
➢ wrist pain;
➢ neck pain;
➢ elbow pain;
➢ tenosynovitis;
➢ peripheral neuropathy;
➢ obesity (due to lack of exercise);
➢ photo-sensitive epilepsy;
➢ increased risk of acute lymphoblastic leukaemia.

Admittedly, these adverse effects are quite rare and 'treatment' simply involves not playing the games in question.

Videogame violence and aggression

One of the main concerns that has constantly been raised against videogames is that most of the games are claimed to feature aggressive elements. This has led some people to state that children become more aggressive after playing such games. However, these assertions have been made without the backup of empirical evidence. Despite the controversy continuing for over 15 years, there has been relatively little systematic research. The issue is more important than ever, because new games are using more explicit and realistic representations of extreme violence.

Theoretically, videogames could have the capacity to promote aggressive tendencies (as predicted by, for example, social learning theory) or to release aggressive tendencies (as predicted by catharsis theory). Put more simply, social learning theory would suggest that playing aggressive videogames leads to the stimulation of aggressive behaviour (i.e. children will imitate what they see on screen). In direct contradiction to this, catharsis theory would suggest that the playing of aggressive videogames would channel latent aggression and therefore have a positive effect on a child's behaviour. The rest of this section briefly examines the growing body of research that has been carried out, by type of study, in order to put the debate into an empirical context.

Self-report methods

The presence of increased aggression has been measured by self-report questionnaires in a number of studies (e.g. Griffiths and Hunt, 1995). Many of the results are contradictory, with some showing that violent videogames have a calming effect whereas others claim violent videogames increase aggression and hostility scores. The problem with all questionnaire research is that correlational evidence is unconvincing, not only because correlations may be due to backward causation (i.e. aggressive children may be drawn to videogames rather than their aggression being purely a result of this activity), but also for the more plausible reason that the correlations may result from mediating factors (e.g. low educational attainment or low socio-economic status) that may themselves be causally related both to the playing of videogames and to aggressive behaviour.

Experimental studies

There have been experimental studies looking at the relationship between aggression and the playing of videogames (e.g. Ballard and West, 1996), although some of these have used videogames as an experimental paradigm to investigate other theoretical concerns. Only experimental studies can hope to provide persuasive evidence regarding causality. However, the laboratory studies to date have examined fantasy aggression rather than real aggression. This is somewhat irrelevant, and the increased aggression in the fantasy and role-play measures, far from confirming the hypothesis that games cause aggression, is entirely consistent with the catharsis hypothesis, that is, it might be precisely the fantasy aggression that releases the energy that would otherwise be expressed as aggressive behaviour. Since laboratory studies cannot study serious aggressive behaviour for ethical reasons, what is required are naturalistic field experiments. However, such field experiments have been non-existent up to now in the field of videogame research.

Observational studies

A number of studies have examined the differences in children's behaviour after playing an aggressive videogame by observing the child's free play (e.g. Irwin and Gross, 1995). These studies, all of which were carried out on young children, do seem to suggest that the playing of violent videogames has the effect of increasing a child's aggressive behaviour – at least in the short term. It is possible that this particular methodology may itself be contributing to the effect. For instance, the novelty of the playroom with new toys (including those associated with aggression) may be played with more than if the experiment were done in the child's own setting. Alternatively, this may be a genuine effect which mirrors research showing that young children imitate what they see on television as a common way of reacting and learning (behaviour which diminishes as they get older).

Other studies (projective tests, case studies)

Other studies, of various methodologies (self-report, experiment and observation), have suggested that videogames may have short-term beneficial effects on children. For example, Graybill *et al.* (1987) concluded that their results were more consistent with catharsis theory (i.e. the release of aggressive tendencies): violent videogames discharge aggressive impulses in a socially acceptable way and playing violent videogames may have a short-term beneficial effect for the children playing them. However, longer-term negative effects were not ruled out in any of these studies.

Conclusions

All the studies that have examined the effects of videogames on aggression have involved measures only of possible short-term aggressive consequences.

The majority of the studies on very young children – as opposed to those in their teens upwards – tend to show that children *do* become more aggressive after either playing or watching a violent videogame, but all these studies were based on the observation of a child's free play after playing a violent videogame. Such evidence suggests that, at a theoretical level, there is more empirical evidence supporting social learning theory than catharsis theory – particularly in younger children. However, there is much speculation as to whether the procedures to measure aggression levels are methodologically valid and reliable.

There is also the very important question of developmental effects – do videogames have the same effect regardless of age? It could well be the case – and is probably the case, after reviewing the research evidence – that violent videogames have a more pronounced effect in young children but less of an effect – if any – on children in their teenage years. There is no evidence that violent videogames have any effect on adult behaviour (although it must be pointed out that there are very few studies using adult samples as most of the research has concentrated on children and adolescents).

Moreover, the social context of playing (playing in groups or individually, with or against each other) may affect the results. The findings of some researchers (Anderson and Morrow, 1995) suggest that competitiveness increases aggression. There are also problems concerning the definition of 'violent' or 'aggressive', as there are numerous television cartoons, such as *Tom and Jerry*, which may not be regarded as violent within the operational definitions employed in mass media research. Since all videogames are animated, the same argument might be use for them also. Research into the effects of long-term exposure to videogames on subsequent aggressive behaviour is noticeably lacking and at present remains speculative.

Videogame addiction

The most popular health argument against playing videogames is that it is potentially addictive. According to Soper and Miller (1983), 'videogame addiction' is like any other behavioural addiction and consists of:

➤ a compulsive behavioural involvement;
➤ a lack of interest in other activities;
➤ association mainly with other addicts;
➤ physical and mental symptoms when attempting to stop the behaviour (e.g. the shakes).

Shotton (1989) carried out a study specifically on 'computer addiction' using a sample of 127 people (half being children, half adult; 96% male) who had been self-reportedly 'hooked' on home videogames for at least five years. Seventy-five of these were measured against two control groups and it was reported that the 'computer-dependent' individuals were highly intelligent, motivated and achievement-oriented individuals but often misunderstood. After a five-year follow-up, Shotton found that the younger cohort had done well educationally, attended university and gained high-ranking employment. However, Shotton's research involved people who were familiar with the older generation of videogames, popular in the early 1980s. The videogames of the 1990s may in some way be more psychologically rewarding than 1980s games, in that they require more complex skills and greater dexterity, and feature socially relevant topics and better graphics. Anecdotal accounts of greater psychological rewards could mean that the newer games are more 'addiction inducing', although such an assertion needs empirical backing. Few empirical studies of the addictive nature of videogames have been carried out although limited evidence by Griffiths and Dancaster (1995) suggests that videogame addiction is a function of the game's effects on arousal level.

A recent study examining the videogame playing behaviour of nearly 400 adolescents (aged 12–16 years) (Griffiths and Hunt, 1995, 1998) found that all but five children had played videogames, that almost a third of them played daily and that 7% of them played for at least 30 hours a week. Videogame playing appears to begin at an early age (7–8 years being about the average starting age) and for most children is a fairly harmless activity which takes up little time in their lives and is played purely for fun and enjoyment. However, there does appear to be a small minority of children who play videogames to excess and who could be called 'addicts'. The statistic suggesting that some children may be playing for at least 30 hours a week indicates that anyone interested in the healthy social and educational development of children should be concerned. Similar results have been found in other studies. Furthermore, there have been other reports of behavioural signs of video-game dependency (many which are similar to fruit machine addiction). These have included:

➢ stealing money to play arcade games;
➢ stealing money to buy new games cartridges;
➢ engaging in minor delinquent acts;
➢ using dinner money to play;
➢ truancy in order to play;
➢ not doing homework/getting poor grades;
➢ sacrificing social activities to play;
➢ irritability and annoyance when unable to play;
➢ playing longer than intended;
➢ an increase in self-reported levels of aggression.

The prevalence of 'videogame addiction' among adolescents is still a subject of great controversy. Whether videogames are inherently good or bad is perhaps not the relevant question. We should rather be asking ourselves about the longitudinal effects – of any activity, not just playing videogames, that takes up 30 hours of leisure time a week – on the educational, health and social development of children and adolescents.

It is clear that the negative consequences of playing videogames arise in those individuals who do so excessively. From prevalence studies in this area, there is little evidence of serious acute adverse effects on health from moderate play. Adverse effects are likely to be relatively minor, and temporary, resolving spontaneously with decreased frequency of play, or to affect only a small subgroup of players. Those who play them to excess are the most at risk from developing health problems although, again, more research appears to be required. The need to establish the incidence and prevalence of clinically significant problems associated with the playing of videogames is of paramount importance, as is a more detailed empirical analysis of the conceptual similarities between videogames and gambling and their impact on the lives of adolescents.

Videogames: what can parents do?

Many parents want advice concerning videogames. The Hints for Parents section on p. 55 sets out some guidelines for them. To begin with, they should begin by finding out what videogames their children are actually playing! Parents might find that some of them contain material that they would prefer them not to be exposed to. If they have objections to the content of the games, they should facilitate discussion with their children about this and, if appropriate, have a few rules. Parents' aims with their children should be:

➢ to help them choose suitable games which are still fun;
➢ to talk with them about the content of the games so that they understand the difference between make-believe and reality;
➢ to discourage solitary game playing;
➢ to guard against obsessive playing;
➢ to follow recommendations on the possible risks outlined by videogame manufacturers;
➢ to ensure that they have plenty of other activities to pursue in their free time besides the playing of videogames.

Parents need to remember that, in the right context, videogames can be educational (helping children to think and learn more quickly), can help raise children's self-esteem, and can increase the speed of their reaction times. Parents and teachers can also use videogames as a starting point for other activities like painting, drawing, acting or storytelling. All of these things will help a child at school. Parents need to remember that playing videogames is just one of many activities that a child can do, alongside sporting activities, school clubs, reading and watching the television. These can all contribute to a balanced recreational diet. But when does it become a problem? The most asked question a parent wants answering is 'How much videogame playing is too much?' To help answer this question the following checklist (Griffiths, 1993b) was devised for parents to check whether their child's videogame playing was getting out of hand. Does the child:

➤ Play almost every day?
➤ Often play for long periods (over three hours a time)?
➤ Play for excitement?
➤ Get restless and irritable if unable to play?
➤ Sacrifice social and sporting activities?
➤ Play instead of doing homework?
➤ Try to cut down on playing but can't?

A positive answer to more than four of these questions may suggest that the child is playing too much. So what can parents do if their children do play too much?

First of all, they can check on and regulate the content of the games. They should try to give children games which are educational rather than violent. Parents usually have control over what their children watch on television — videogames should not be any different.

Secondly, they should try to encourage the playing of videogames in groups rather than as a solitary activity. This will lead to children talking and working together.

Thirdly, they should set time limits on children's playing time and, for example, tell them that they can play for a couple of hours after they have done their homework or their chores — not before.

Fourthly, parents should always get their children to follow the recommendations by the videogame manufacturers (e.g. sit at least two feet from the screen, play in a well lit room, never have the screen at maximum brightness, and never play videogames when feeling tired).

Finally, if all else fails, parents can temporarily take away the games console and then give it back to the children on a part-time basis when appropriate.

Conclusions

Case studies reporting the more negative consequences of playing videogames have all involved people who did so to excess. From prevalence studies in this area, there is little evidence of serious acute adverse effects on health from moderate play. Adverse effects are likely to be relatively minor, and temporary, resolving spontaneously with decreased frequency of play, or to affect only a small subgroup of players. Those who play these games to excess are the most at risk of developing health problems, although more research appears to be much needed. As mentioned previously, the need to establish the incidence and prevalence of clinically significant problems associated with videogame play is of paramount importance. There is also no doubt that clearer operational definitions are required if this is to be achieved.

If care is taken in the design, and if they are put into the right context, videogames have the potential to be used as training aids in classrooms and therapeutic settings, and to provide skills in psychomotor coordination in simulations of real-life events (e.g. training recruits for the armed forces). There is, however, a need for a general taxonomy of videogames, as it could be the case that particular types of games have very positive effects while other types are not so positive. The list below, largely based on youngsters' own categorizations of videogames, formulates such a taxonomy:

➢ *Sport simulations.* This type is self-explanatory. These games (e.g. *World Wide Soccer '97, NHL Powerplay '97*) simulate sports such as golf, ice hockey or athletics.
➢ *Racers.* This type could be considered a type of 'sport simulation' in that it simulates motor sports like Formula 1 racing (e.g. *Human Grand Prix, Speedster, Motoracer*).
➢ *Adventures.* This type uses fantasy settings in which the player can escape to other worlds and take on new identities (e.g. *Atlantis, Star Trek Generations, Overboard*).
➢ *Puzzlers.* This type is self-explanatory. These games (e.g. *Tetris, Baku Baku Animal*) are 'brainteasers' which often require active thinking.
➢ *Miscellaneous.* These games (e.g. *Sim City 2000, Populous 3*) are simply those that do not easily fit into any other category.
➢ *Platformers.* These games (e.g. *Mario 64, Sonic*) involve running and jumping along and onto platforms.
➢ *Platform blasters.* These games (e.g. *Robocop 2, Virtua Cop*) are 'platformers' but also involve blasting everything that comes into sight.
➢ *Beat 'Em Ups.* These games (e.g. *Street Fighter 3, Tekken 2, Mortal Kombat*) involve physical violence (punching, kicking).

➤ *Shoot 'Em Ups.* These games (e.g. *Blast Corps, Mech Warrior, Turok Dinosaur Hunter*) involve shooting and killing using various weapons.

As the list shows, there are many different types of videogame, each of which has its own distinctive qualities. Only three of these categories ('beat 'em ups', 'shoot 'em ups' and 'platform blasters') have any kind of aggressive element. If children and adolescents work with this degree of definitional refinement, it follows that other interested parties (e.g. educationalists and researchers) should do also.

Taking all factors and variables into account and considering the prevalence of play, the evidence of serious adverse effects on health is slight. An overview of the available literature appears to indicate that adverse effects are likely to affect only a very small subgroup of players and that frequent players are the most at risk of developing health problems. Those that these games do affect will experience subtle, relatively minor, and temporary effects which resolve spontaneously with decreased frequency of play. However, the possible long-term effects of these games and their relationships to conditions such as obesity have not been fully examined and must remain speculative.

Part VII: Fruit machines and videogames — some final comments

It is clear that excessive involvement with fruit machines and videogames may bring problems to the individual concerned and that these problems appear to be intensified when the individual is an adolescent. The risk factors involved in problem adolescent gambling are beginning to be established, although more research is needed to identify risk factors for the excessive playing of videogames. Without early and appropriate prevention, intervention and treatment, adolescents will become high-risk candidates for developing a variety of dysfunctional behaviours, including a range of addictive behaviour patterns.

It would appear that situational characteristics impact most on the acquisition of excessive playing on fruit machines and videogames, and that structural characteristics impact most on development and maintenance of this behaviour. Furthermore, the most important of these factors appear to be the accessibility of the activity and event frequency (both of which are critical to the success of fruit machines and videogames). It is when these two characteristics combine that the greatest problems could occur. This is well demonstrated by the worldwide proliferation of fruit machines (and the associated problems that go with them). As Griffiths (1999) points out, it could be that gambling on fruit machines has more 'gambling inducing' structural characteristics (as a result of the inherent technology) than other forms of gambling, and could be why a relatively large minority of gamblers in the UK are 'addicted' to fruit machines (many of whom are adolescents). With their integrated mix of conditioning effects, rapid event frequency, short reward intervals and psychological rewards, it is not hard to see how gambling on fruit machines and playing videogames can become repetitive habits.

References

Anderson, C.A. and Morrow, M. (1995). Competitive aggression without interaction: effects of competitive versus cooperative instructions on aggressive behavior in video games. *Personality and Social Psychology Bulletin, 21*, 1020–1030.

Ballard, M.E. and West, J.R. (1996). The effects of violent videogame play on males' hostility and cardiovascular responding. *Journal of Applied Social Psychology*, 26, 717–730.

Bellringer, P. (1993). *Working With Young Problem Gamblers: Guidelines To Practice*. London: UK Forum on Young People and Gambling.

Bellringer, P. (1999). *Understanding Problem Gamblers*. London: Free Association Books.

Bellringer, P. and Farman, J. (1997). *Young Gambling: A Guide For Parents*. London: GamCare.

Deheger, M., Rolland-Cachera, M.F. and Fontvielle, A.M. (1997). Physical activity and body composition in 10 year old French children: Linkages with nutritional intake? *International Journal of Obesity, 21*, 372–379.

Fisher, S. E. (1992). Measuring pathological gambling in children: The case of fruit machines in the U.K. *Journal of Gambling Studies, 8*, 263–285.

Fisher, S. (1993). The pull of the fruit machine: A sociological typology of young players. *Sociological Review, 41*, 446–474.

Fisher, S.E. and Balding, J. (1998). *Gambling and Problem Gambling Among Young People in England and Wales*. London: Office of the National Lottery.

Fisher, S. and Bellringer, P. (1997). *The Young Fruit Machine Player*. London: UK Forum on Young People and Gambling.

Fisher, S.E. and Griffiths, M.D. (1995). Current trends in slot machine gambling: Research and policy issues. *Journal of Gambling Studies, 11*, 239–247.

Gardner, J.E. (1991). Can the Mario Bros help? Nintendo games as an adjunct in psychotherapy with children. *Psychotherapy*, 28, 667–670.

Graf, W.D., Chatrian, G.E., Glass, S.T. and Knauss, T.A. (1994). Video-game related seizures: a report on 10 patients and a review of the literature. *Pediatrics, 3*, 551–556.

Graybill, D., Strawniak, M., Hunter, T. and O'Leary, M. (1987). Effects of playing versus observing violent versus non-violent video games on children's aggression. *Psychology, A Quarterly Journal of Human Behavior, 24*, 1–7.

Griffiths, M.D. (1989). Gambling in children and adolescents. *Journal of Gambling Behavior, 5*, 66–83.

Griffiths, M.D. (1990). Addiction to fruit machines: a preliminary study among males. *Journal of Gambling Studies, 6*, 113–126.

Griffiths, M.D. (1991a). Amusement machine playing in childhood and adolescence: a comparative analysis of video games and fruit machines. *Journal of Adolescence, 14*, 53–73.

Griffiths, M.D. (1991b). The observational analysis of adolescent gambling in UK amusement arcades. *Journal of Community and Applied Social Psychology, 1*, 309–320.

Griffiths, M.D. (1991c). Fruit machine addiction: two brief case studies. *British Journal of Addiction, 85*, 465.

Griffiths, M.D. (1992). Pinball wizard: a case study of a pinball addict. *Psychological Reports, 71*, 160–162.

Griffiths, M.D. (1993a). Fruit machine gambling: the importance of structural characteristics. *Journal of Gambling Studies, 9*, 101–120.

Griffiths, M.D. (1993b). *Your Child and Video Games: Advice for Parents*. Coventry: National Council for Educational Technology (leaflet).

Griffiths, M.D. (1994a). Co-existent fruit machine addiction and solvent abuse: a cause for concern? *Journal of Adolescence, 17*, 491–498.

Griffiths, M.D. (1994b). The role of cognitive bias and skill in fruit machine gambling. *British Journal of Psychology, 85*, 351–369.

Griffiths, M.D. (1995a). Technological addictions. *Clinical Psychology Forum, 76*, 14–19.

Griffiths, M.D. (1995b). *Adolescent Gambling*. London: Routledge.

Griffiths, M.D. (1996a). Behavioural addictions: an issue for everybody. *Employee Counselling Today, 8(3)*, 19–25.

Griffiths, M.D. (1996b). Nicotine, tobacco and addiction. *Nature, 384*, 18.

Griffiths, M.D. (1999). Gambling technologies: prospects for problem gambling. *Journal of Gambling Studies, 15*, 265–283.

Griffiths, M.D. and Dancaster, I. (1995). The effect of Type A personality on physiological arousal while playing computer games. *Addictive Behaviors, 20*, 543–548.

Griffiths, M.D. and Hunt, N. (1995). Computer game playing in adolescence: prevalence and demographic indicators. *Journal of Community and Applied Social Psychology, 5*, 189–194.

Griffiths, M.D. and Hunt, N. (1998). Dependence on computer game playing by adolescents. *Psychological Reports, 82*, 475–480.

Griffiths, M.D. and Sutherland, I. (1998). Adolescent gambling and drug use. *Journal of Community and Applied Social Psychology, 8*, 423–427.

Griffiths, M.D. and Wood, R.T.A. (1999). *Lottery gambling and addiction: An Overview of European Research.* Lausanne: Association of European Lotteries.

Gwinup, G., Haw, T. and Elias, A. (1983). Cardiovascular changes in video game players: cause for concern? *Postgraduate Medicine, 74*, 245.

Hatch, E.E., Linet, M.S., Kleinerman, R.A., *et al.* (1998). Association between childhood acute lymphoblastic leukemia and use of electrical appliances during pregnancy and childhood. *Epidemiology, 9*, 234–245.

Irwin, A.R. and Gross, A.M. (1995). Cognitive tempo, violent video games, and aggressive behavior in young boys. *Journal of Family Violence, 10*, 337–350.

Johnson, B. and Hackett, A.F. (1997). Eating habits of 11–14-year-old schoolchildren living in less affluent areas of Liverpool, UK. *Journal of Human Nutrition and Dietetics, 10*, 135–144.

Keisler, S., Sproull, L. and Eccles, J.S. (1983). Second class citizens. *Psychology Today, 17(3)*, 41–48.

Malone, T.W. (1981). Toward a theory of intrinsically motivating instruction. *Cognitive Science, 4*, 333–369.

Marlatt, G.A., Baer, J.S., Donovan, D.M. and Kivlahan, D.R. (1988). Addictive behaviors: etiology and treatment. *Annual Review of Psychology, 39*, 223–252.

McIlwraith, R., Jacobvitz, R.S., Kubey, R. and Alexander, A. (1991). Television addiction: theories and data behind the ubiquitous metaphor. *American Behavioral Scientist, 35*, 104–121.

Millett, C.J., Fish, D.R. and Thompson, P.J. (1997). A survey of epilepsy-patient perceptions of video-game material/electronic screens and other factors as seizure precipitants. *Seizure, 6*, 457–459.

Murphy, J.K., Stoney, C.M., Alpert, B.S. and Walker, S.S. (1995). Gender and ethnicity in children's cardiovascular reactivity: 7 years of study. *Health Psychology, 14*, 48–55.

Orford, J. (1985). *Excessive Appetites: A Psychological View of the Addictions.* Chichester: Wiley.

Scheibe, K.E. and Erwin, M. (1979). The computer as altar. *Journal of Social Psychology, 108*, 103–109.

Segal, K.R. and Dietz, W.H. (1991). Physiologic responses to playing a video game. *American Journal of Diseases of Children, 145*, 1034–1036.

Selnow, G.W. (1984). Playing video games: the electronic friend. *Journal of Communication, 34*, 148–156.

Shimai, S., Yamada, F., Masuda, K. and Tada, M. (1993). TV game play and obesity in Japanese school children. *Perceptual and Motor Skills, 76*, 1121–1122.

Shotton, M. (1989). *Computer Addiction? A Study of Computer Dependency.* London: Taylor and Francis.

Soper, W.B. and Miller, M.J. (1983). Junk time junkies: an emerging addiction among students. *School Counsellor, 31*, 40–43.

Wanner, E. (1982). The electronic bogeyman. *Psychology Today, 16(10)*, 8–11.

Wood, R.T.A. and Griffiths, M.D. (1998). The acquisition, development and maintenance of lottery and scratchcard gambling in adolescence. *Journal of Adolescence, 21*, 265–273.

Yeoman, T. and Griffiths, M.D. (1996). Adolescent machine gambling and crime. *Journal of Adolescence, 19*, 183–188.

Further reading

Blaszczynski, A. (1998). *Overcoming Compulsive Gambling.* London: Robinson Books.

Griffiths, M.D. (1995). *Adolescent Gambling.* London: Routledge.

Willans, A. (1996). *Gambling – A Family Affair.* London: Sheldon Press.

Appendices

Appendix 1. Diagnostic checklist to identify problem gambling in children and adolescents

These questions are based on DSM–IV-J questions (see Fisher, 1992). If a person answers 'yes' to four or more of the following, they may have a gambling problem.

1. Do you find yourself thinking about fruit machines at odd times of day or planning the next time that you will play?
2. Do you find you need to spend more and more money on playing fruit machines?
3. Do you become restless, tense, fed up, or bad tempered when trying to cut down or stop playing fruit machines?
4. Do you play fruit machines as a way of escaping your problems?
5. After spending money on fruit machines, do you play again another day to try to win your money back (more than half the time)?
6. Do you lie to your family or friends to hide how much you play fruit machines?
7a. In the past year have you spent your school dinner money, or money for bus or train fares, on fruit machines?
7b. In the past year have you taken money from someone you live with, without their knowing, to play fruit machines?
7c. In the past year have you stolen money from outside the family, or shoplifted, to play fruit machines?
8a. Have you fallen out with members of your family, or close friends, because of playing fruit machines?
8b. In the past year have you missed school to play fruit machines (five times or more)?
9. In the past year have you gone to somebody for help with a serious money worry caused by playing fruit machines?

Appendix 2. Early warning signs of a gambling addiction

➢ Unexplained absences from home.
➢ Continual lying about day-to-day movements.
➢ Constant shortage of money.
➢ General increase in secretiveness.
➢ Neglect of studies, family, friends, health and appearance.
➢ Agitation (if unable to gamble).
➢ Mood swings.
➢ Loss of friends and social life.
➢ Gambling seen as a legitimate way of making money.

Appendix 3. Signs of a definite gambling problem

➢ Large debts (which are always explained away).
➢ Trouble at school or college about non-attendance.
➢ Unexplained borrowing from family and friends.
➢ Unwillingness to repay borrowed money.
➢ Total preoccupation with gambling and spending money on gambling.
➢ Gambling alone for long periods.
➢ Constantly chasing losses in an attempt to win money back.
➢ Constantly gambling until all money is gone.
➢ Complete alienation and rejection from family and friends.
➢ Lying about the extent of their gambling to family and friends.
➢ Committing crimes as a way of getting money for gambling or paying off debts.
➢ Gambling overriding all other interests and obligations.

Appendix 4. Profile of the problem adolescent gambler

➤ Unwilling to accept reality and has a lack of responsibility for gambling.
➤ Gambles to escape deeper problems (and the gambling environment may even be a substitute for parental affection).
➤ Insecure and feels inferior to parents and elders.
➤ Wants good things without making an effort and loves games of chance.
➤ Likes to be a 'big shot' and feels it is important to win (gambling offers status and a way of defining achievement).
➤ Likes to compete.
➤ Feels guilty, with losses acting as a punishing behaviour.
➤ May be depressed.
➤ Low self-esteem and confidence.
➤ Other compulsive and addictive traits.

Appendix 5. Useful addresses for sources of help and information about youth gambling

GamCare

25–27 Catherine Place, Westminster, London SW1E 6DU.
Tel: 0207 233 8988; Fax: 0207 233 8977
E-mail: director@gamcare.org.uk; website: www.gamcare.org.uk

GamCare is the national centre for information, advice and practical help in relation to the social impact of gambling. It provides a national telephone helpline (0845 6000 133) and a face-to-face counselling service. It also produces a wide range of educational materials on gambling and problem gambling.

Gamblers Anonymous/Gam-Anon

PO Box 88, London SW10 0EU.
Tel: 0207 384 3040 (helpline)

Gamblers Anonymous (GA) is a self-help fellowship which has over 200 groups throughout the country. Gam-Anon is the 'sister' organization to GA and provides support and advice to partners and parents of problem gamblers. Literature available on request.

Gordon House Association

186 Mackenzie Road, Beckenham, Kent BR3 4SF
Tel: 0208 778 3331.

The Gordon House Association provides residential facilities for male problem gamblers over the age of 18 years. There are a limited number of beds although a second hostel is now open in Dudley (West Midlands).

Parents of Young Gamblers

Tel: 0121 443 2609

This a telephone helpline which provides verbal advice and information about youth gambling.

Other services

Local counselling services may also be able to help. Check a local telephone directory for details or speak to a general practitioner.

Appendix 6. Practitioner interventions for gambling dependency

The following guidelines (adapted from the GamCare leaflet *Interventions for Gambling Dependency: A Guide for Practitioners or Those Supporting a Problem Gambler*) may be used to provide effective help for the problem gambler. They are drawn from a range of practical approaches. To be effective, there needs to be absolute honesty and a degree of genuine motivation by the gambler. There also needs a mutual acceptance and agreement of all tasks and targets.

1. Understand the issues

Gain what knowledge you can (positive or negative) about the issues of gambling.

2. Structure change

Adapt a method of changing behaviour you have used with other problems (e.g. alcohol and drug problems), or develop one that is realistic and attainable.

3. Assess the problem

A thorough assessment is needed to ascertain what the problem is, whose problem it is and how much is 'owned' by the gambler (i.e. does the gambler accept and take responsibility for the problem?)

4. Offer counselling

High-quality counselling may be beneficial for the gambler both on a one-to-one basis and involving others in group (e.g. family) therapy.

5. Develop trust

It is important to develop a trusting relationship between yourself and the gambler, and between the family and peers of the gambler.

6. Build self-esteem

The gambler's self-esteem will almost certainly be low and will need sensitive handling.

7. Provide support

Establish effective support systems for the gambler to call upon, such as a network of support involving family and friends, and an inter-agency network.

8. Manage finances

Debt counselling will almost certainly be needed, and the control and accountability of all money may be required. If mutually agreed, it can help a gambler initially if a trusted friend or family member holds finances until the gambler's confidence in managing money is restored.

9. Develop interests

Dependency on gambling must be replaced by a range of activities and interests that will meet similar needs. Often sports or other activities which have a strong element of risk or competition are appropriate (e.g. football, outdoor pursuits).

10. Measure progress

Throughout the process of working with the gambler, assess and measure progress. If you mutually agree tasks or a contract, progress is easy to see.

Appendix 7. Self-help guide for young gamblers: strategies for change

The following (adapted from the GamCare leaflets *A Sure Bet? Self-help Guide for Young Gamblers* and *Easy Come, Easy Go? Self-help Guide for Problem Gamblers*) are some practical steps to help you overcome a problem with gambling.

Tell someone

➤ Talk to someone that you trust – this could be a friend, family member, probation officer or treatment professional.
➤ Don't run away from your problems. Take responsibility for your actions and start addressing the problems whatever they are (debt, deceit, criminal activity, relationship problems). Be honest first with yourself, then with other people.

Practical steps

➤ Stop all gambling while trying to overcome your problem gambling.
➤ Get professional help. For instance, counselling provides a confidential way to talk over all your worries and problems.
➤ If possible join a self-help group. Talking to others in a similar position to yourself can be incredibly supportive.
➤ Record your feelings in a diary. If you have avoided gambling, write down how you are feeling and how you have coped. If you have been unable to stop gambling, write down the events that led up to the gambling episode(s). Record your feelings before, during and after.
➤ Look for patterns in your behaviour. Do you gamble out of boredom? Do you gamble because you feel stressed or under pressure? Do you gamble after family arguments? Write these in your diary.
➤ Record each day that you do not gamble on a calendar. This provides an easy to see visual marker of your progress. If you have a 'slip', use the calendar to see how long you abstained. Set a target to beat that number.

Money

➤ Manage your money. If you have a cashpoint card, then cut it up or give it to someone you trust to look after it for you.
➤ Ask someone you trust to handle your money for an agreed period of time. When the time is up, review whether you are ready to retake control of your finances.

Managing change

➢ Give yourself a reward after a period free from gambling by spending some of the money you have saved on yourself. Buy something personal and unrelated to gambling. Take a friend with you if you are uncomfortable about handling money.

➢ Take one day at a time, as this will make it easier to break your gambling habit.

Distractions

➢ Be prepared to get withdrawal symptoms. For instance, you may get hot and cold sweats, palpitations, feel shaky or feel unusually moody, irritable and depressed.

➢ When you get the urge to gamble, talk to someone or find something to distract you until the urge subsides.

➢ Increase your range of other interests, especially those that involve other people. Try to do things with friends and family who are not gamblers.

➢ A gambling dependency must be replaced by activities and interests that meet similar needs. You could try sports or other competitive and risk-taking activities (outdoor pursuits, bungee jumping, football, etc.)

Be positive

➢ The key to stopping your gambling is to ensure that any change is manageable and realistic. Each goal that you achieve will help you grow in confidence and self-esteem. This will also provide the incentive to reach your next goal.

➢ If you have a 'slip', do not punish yourself. Stopping a gambling dependency is very difficult. Instead, reflect on your 'slip' and think about what you have learned from it.

➢ Be optimistic. Almost everyone can overcome a gambling dependency and go on to lead a normal life. Some gamblers find it impossible to go back to gambling without losing control, while others at a later stage are able to return to controlled gambling.

Appendix 8. The 'good gambling' guide for adolescents

These guidelines will help ensure that gambling remains an enjoyable and problem-free experience.

➢ When you are gambling you are buying entertainment, not investing money.
➢ You are unlikely to make money from gambling.
➢ The gaming industry and the government are the real winners.
➢ You should gamble only with money that you can afford to lose.
➢ You should set strict limits on how much you will gamble.
➢ To make profit from gambling you should quit when ahead.
➢ Gambling should take up only a small amount of your time and interest.
➢ Problems will arise if you become preoccupied with gambling.
➢ Gambling within your means can be a fun and exciting activity.
➢ Gambling outside your means is likely to create serious problems.
➢ You should not gamble to escape from worries or pressures.
➢ The feeling of being powerful and in control when gambling is a delusion.
➢ A gambling dependency is as damaging as other addictions.
➢ Always gamble responsibly.

Appendix 9. Types of gaming machine

There are basically three types of gaming machine (all of which are potentially addictive):

Amusement with prize (AWP) machines – commonly known as fruit machines. These are found on many premises including pubs, cafes, amusement arcades, motorway service stations and cinema foyers. Fruit machines have no legal restrictions although many premises have voluntary restrictions ('No under-18s', 'No under-16s', 'Children must be accompanied by an adult', etc.). There are also 'all cash' fruit machines (most commonly found in pubs and betting shops), where players must be over 18 years of age to participate.

Jackpot machines – these are almost identical to fruit machines but have bigger initial stakes and much bigger payouts. These are found in registered clubs which have a gaming licence and players must be over 18 years of age.

Videogame machines and other electronic machines – these machines are unlicensed and can be found on many premises just like AWPs. They can take the form of videogames, trivia quiz machines or pinball machines, for example.

Hints for parents

How parents can support a problem gambler

The guidelines for parents are adapted from the GamCare leaflet *Supporting a Problem Gambler: A Guide for Parents, Partners and Relatives*.

➢ Remember that you are not the only family facing this problem.
➢ You may be able to help your child by talking the problem through, but it is probably better if a skilled person outside the family is also involved.
➢ Keep in mind that it is a serious matter and that your child cannot 'just give up' gambling.
➢ Take a firm stand. While it might feel easier to give in to demands and to believe everything your child says, this allows your child to avoid facing the problem.
➢ Remember that your child likes to gamble and is getting something from the activity quite apart from money.
➢ Do not forget that gamblers are good at lying – to themselves as well as others.
➢ Let your child know that you believe it is a problem even though your child may not admit it.
➢ Encourage your child all the time, as it is important to be motivated to change.
➢ Be prepared to accept that your child may not be motivated to change until faced with an acute crisis.
➢ Leave the responsibility for gambling and its consequences with the gambler, but also help your child to face up to it and to work at overcoming the dependency.
➢ Do not condemn your child, as it is likely to be unhelpful and may drive lead to further gambling.
➢ Setting firm and fair boundaries for your child's behaviour is appropriate and is likely to be constructive in providing a framework with which to address the dependency.
➢ Despite what your child may have done it is important to say that you still love them. This should be done even if you have to make a 'tough love' decision such as asking your child to leave home.
➢ Do not trust your child with money until the dependency has been broken. If they are agreeable it is a helpful strategy for a defined short

period of time to manage their money for them. In addition, help develop their financial management skills.

➤ Encourage your child to try other activities – try to identify other activities that the child is good at and encourage those.

➤ Give praise for any achievements (however small) although don't go over the top.

➤ Provide opportunities to contribute to the family or the running of the house, to encourage the development of responsibility.

➤ Try to listen with understanding and look at your child with pleasure. Communication channels between child and parent can easily be blocked so simple measures can pay big dividends.

➤ Bear in mind that as a parent you will need support, too, through this long process of helping the child. You will need the support of your family and may also need additional support from a helping agency.

Videogames: what can parents do?

To begin with, find out what videogames your children are actually playing! You might find that some of them contain material that they would prefer them not to be exposed to. If you object to the content of the games, you should discussion this with your children. If appropriate, have a few rules. Your aims with your children should be:

➤ to help them choose suitable games which are still fun;

➤ to talk with them about the content of the games so that they understand the difference between make-believe and reality;

➤ to discourage solitary game playing;

➤ to guard against obsessive playing;

➤ to follow recommendations on the possible risks outlined by videogame manufacturers;

➤ to ensure that they have plenty of other activities to pursue in their free time besides the playing of videogames.

Remember that, in the right context, videogames can be educational (helping children to think and learn more quickly), can help raise children's self-esteem, and can increase their speed of their reaction times. Remember though that playing videogames is just one of many activities that a child can do, alongside sporting activities, school clubs, reading and watching the television.

How much videogame playing is too much?

The following checklist will help you to check whether your child's video-game playing is getting out of hand. Ask these simple questions. Does your child:

➢ Play almost every day?
➢ Often play for long periods (over three hours a time)?
➢ Play for excitement?
➢ Get restless and irritable if unable to play?
➢ Sacrifice social and sporting activities?
➢ Play instead of doing homework?
➢ Try to cut down on playing but can't?

If the answer is 'yes' to more than four of these questions, your the child may be playing too much.

What you can do if your children play too much

➢ Check on and regulate the content of the games.
➢ Give your children games which are educational rather than violent.
➢ Try to encourage the playing of videogames in groups rather than alone.
➢ Set time limits on children's playing time and, for example, tell them that they can play for a couple of hours after they have done their homework or their chores – not before.
➢ Always get your children to follow the recommendations by the video-game manufacturers – to sit at least two feet from the screen, play in a well lit room, never have the screen at maximum brightness and never play videogames when feeling tired.
➢ If all else fails, temporarily take away the games console and then give it back to the children on a part-time basis when appropriate.